Monster's Baking Day

Written by David Orme
Illustrated by Lorraine White

Collins Educational
An Imprint of HarperCollins*Publishers*

Monster loved baking cakes.

He was having a baking day.

The postman looked in.

"That smells good," said the postman.

Monster gave him a slice.

Monster sang.

The dustman was passing.
"That smells good," said the dustman.

Monster gave him a slice.

Monster sang.

The paper girl rode past.
She heard Monster sing.

"That smells good,"
said the paper girl.

Monster gave her a slice.

Monster sang.

There was just one slice left.

The window cleaner came by.
She looked through the window.

“That does smell good,”
said the window cleaner.

Monster gave her the last slice.

Monster sang sadly.

The plate was empty.

said Monster.

And he ate the other cake as
quickly as he could before
anyone else came by.